The New Entrepreneur

The New Entrepreneur

Your Action Guide to Business Development

Yolanda **Ceasar**

THE NEW ENTREPRENEUR
YOUR ACTION GUIDE TO BUSINESS DEVELOPMENT

iUniverse books may be ordered through booksellers or by contacting:

iUniverse
1663 Liberty Drive
Bloomington, IN 47403
www.iuniverse.com
1-800-Authors (1-800-288-4677)

Because of the dynamic nature of the Internet, any web addresses or links contained in this book may have changed since publication and may no longer be valid. The views expressed in this work are solely those of the author and do not necessarily reflect the views of the publisher, and the publisher hereby disclaims any responsibility for them.

Any people depicted in stock imagery provided by Thinkstock are models, and such images are being used for illustrative purposes only. Certain stock imagery © Thinkstock.

ISBN: 978-1-5320-0318-9 (sc)
ISBN: 978-1-5320-0319-6 (e)

Library of Congress Control Number: 2016911634

Print information available on the last page.

iUniverse rev. date: 10/14/2016

Contents

Introduction

Nothing is more rewarding than creating your own business. Financial freedom is only one of the many rewards of entrepreneurship. However, the burden and financial responsibility of a business start-up can deter one from venturing out and seeking autonomy over his or her own life. The highs and lows—along with the joys and disappointments—all add to the plethora of wisdom that one gains through experience when carrying out his or her vision. It is imperative that every dream is evaluated properly and well thought out before implementation can begin.

I have designed this step-by-step action guide to help you develop and execute the vision of your business. The objectives and goals of this action guide are to allow as much of your own thoughts, ideas, and visions to be written down and laid out in plain view. In doing so you will be able to organize your thoughts, monitor your progress, and follow through on your process as your vision begins to unfold and manifest in your life.

The struggle for many is not so much the idea, but the how to get it done. I have designed this straightforward guide to be quick to the punch in order to further assist in the development of your venture. Self-development, which involves the reading of relevant books, is highly important during this journey so you may prepare your mind-set for the highs and lows that all leaders experience. The key to it all is consistency.

As an entrepreneur, I understand the determination needed for this venture. For me, it was a no-brainer. But it took a lot of dedication, sacrifice, and time spent toward the vision that was imparted into me. Understanding my purpose, passion, and leadership role helped transform my mind from a dependent to independent role.

But the transformation did not occur overnight. It took years. When I initially graduated from college, I became a licensed practical nurse (LPN), where I operated in a dependent role under the supervision of a registered nurse (RN).

The RN oversees all decisions that may affect the outcome of the patient's general well-being. The decisions that an LPN makes are based on the ones that the RN implemented. Any deviations from the original decision must go through the RN, who creates and develops the plan of care while an LPN makes sure it is implemented.

I was told early in my career, "An LPN is paid for what she does; an RN is paid for what she thinks." So naturally I returned to nursing school to get paid for what I think.

During my advanced nursing training, I learned the art of becoming a critical thinker. This is a difficult skill to learn, especially for me because I have always had someone to go to if I had any problems or if the weight of the burdens being presented to me became too heavy. Now as an RN, the only person I could go to for help is another experienced RN or physician. If the physician does not know the answer, I have to think for us both because we are a team. The moral of the story is that the employee is the LPN (dependent role) and the business owner is the RN (independent role).

If you take nothing else from this action guide, grab the knowledge that it is important to acquire and possess the skill of a critical thinker. This is essential to the survival of your business. Please think about each question when you begin to make your dreams become a reality.

Chapter 1

What Is a Business?

Let us define the word *business*. It can be "an occupation, profession, or trade and includes the purchase and sale of goods in an attempt to make a profit. It involves a person, corporation, or partnership that is engaged in manufacturing of a product or service in hopes of gaining a profit." The company leaders' character solely determines the dynamics and ethics of a business' operation.

Before starting the venture of constructing your business dream, you must spend time educating yourself about the craft of your desired industry. As a leader it is imperative that you constantly invest in yourself via self-development.

What Is a Leader?

A leader is a guiding or directing head, a person or thing that leads. Leaders are set apart from everyone else. They are groomed and must possess stamina, character, and integrity. A good place to start in character building and development is reading books on leadership. Use the following reading log to record your books as you develop your library.

My Library

- Book 1
- Book 2
- Book 3
- Book 4
- Book 5
- Book 6

Character Building

The terms used in this chapter are defined as follows:

- Integrity: adherence to moral and ethical principles
- Character: the combination of qualities or features that distinguishes one person, group, or thing from another
- Morals: of or concerned with the judgment of the goodness or badness of human action and character

Books on Integrity

- Book 1
- Book 2
- Book 3
- Book 4
- Book 5

Goal Setting

Emerging leaders must understand the importance of setting goals. A goal is a byproduct, achievement, or result toward which effort is directed. Becoming goal-oriented or outcome-driven are key factors in developing a leader's mind-set. Setting goals is a powerful tool that is at the root of business principles. Goal-oriented leaders understand that, not only does setting goals help with motivating themselves, it can be used to help inspire others.

When setting goals, they must be SMART, or specific, measurable, attainable, relevant, and time-bound.

Specific

When it comes to setting goals, they must be precise. Understanding this is important for the desired outcome to be produced. When we set unclear goals, it is likely to cause frustration and apprehension. To set a specific goal, ask yourself, "Who? What? When? Where? Why? How?"

Measurable

Goals must be measurable or have the ability to be measured. This simply means that the goal can be counted. For example, you say, "I want to read five books on building character in forty days." This goal is specific in what type of book. It gives the amount of books you want to read, and it is time-bound.

Attainable

When a goal is attainable, it has the capability of being achieved or met. When setting goals, the objective should be realistic and reachable. For example, if you set a goal to lose twenty pounds in twenty-four hours, that is unrealistic and unattainable. Using the goal mentioned in the previous section as an example, it is attainable because it is possible to read five books on building character in forty days. If you give yourself five to seven days to read one book, you will easily meet this goal.

Relevant

The goal must be applicable. If you are working on building character, it is nonsensical to include a horror novel in one of your five books. Remember that every step you make must be directed toward reaching your goal.

Time-bound

This means your goals must have a deadline. If you do not reach your objective in the specific amount of time, it was not met. It is okay to go back and reevaluate your deadline to see if it were the reason the goal was not attainable.

Write down your goals and set a reasonable time frame to obtain them. Each chapter will have a section for setting goals to help you stay on task.

Setting Goals: Character Building

Goal #1

I will read ___ (amount) of books on leadership and character in _____ (time frame).

Book 1:_____ Date Completed:_____

Book 2:_____ Date Completed:_____

Book 3:_____ Date Completed:_____

Book 4:_____ Date Completed:_____

Book 5:_____ Date Completed:_____

Did you meet the above goal?

Chapter 2

Where Do I Begin?

After you have spent some time building character and developing self, you can now focus on what is next. In this chapter you will discover what you can offer. The objective here is to discover your passion, determine if what you have to offer can turn into a business, and make the first step in business development.

This is the fun part. Can you imagine making a living doing something you love? Learning to develop the entrepreneur in you is one of the reasons you are following this action guide. An entrepreneur organizes, manages, and develops an organization or enterprise of any kind. Entrepreneurs solve problems, and they are critical thinkers. They see a puzzle or picture and work from the end to the beginning instead of working from the beginning to the end.

Envision your finished product or project. What does it look like? What colors are involved? Whom are you selling it to? Do you see a crowd buying into it? Now imagine all the things that could possibly go wrong and work from there.

When putting your business together, you must ask yourself these questions:

- Who is my target audience?
- Does my service or product meet my target audience's needs?
- What is the age group of my target audience?
- What are the demographics of my target audience: age, sex, salary earnings, area of residence, education level, race/creed, and/or religion?

By answering these questions, you are now formulating a plan. You can use the information above in your business plan. Be sure to think analytically when answering these questions.

What Type of Business Will It Be?

Your business can be a trade, for-profit, nonprofit, service-oriented, or product-oriented. You should make the decision based on what you are trying to do and your knowledge base of the area you are starting a business in.

Trade is the action of buying and selling goods and services. A for-profit business is a corporation that is intended to operate a business that will return a profit to the owner. A nonprofit organization is retained for its self-preservation, expansion, or plans, even though some profit surplus is allowed. Finally a product is anything produced, created, or designed by the labor of a person or machine. It is a tangible, valuable item that solves the problems and/or meets the consumer's needs.

Here you can identify the product you plan to sell or trade in your business:

Product List

- Product
- Product
- Product
- Product
- Product

Will you be selling or trading your product? What is the name of your product? Will your product solve the problem or meet the needs of your target consumer?

A service provides work for an individual or business. It often requires someone to be present to carry out the task being sold. A service can create a good business, but it is often limited to where you (the person providing the service resides) or where the company is located in the country or world. Always remember that products can go where you cannot and can reach those you cannot and are more likely to make you wealthy.

Finally ask yourself the following questions:

- What services will I offer?
- Who will be providing the services?
- What time will I be providing the services?
- Is there a need for the services I will be offering in the area I will provide them?
- Is equipment required to carry out these services? If so, what kind?

- If any equipment is needed, where will it be obtained?
- Can I rent the equipment? For how much?

Once you have discovered your passion and formulated a plan, it is a good idea to frequently review what you have written to ensure you stay on task.

Chapter 3

Develop Your Brand

In this chapter you will learn what branding is. The objectives of branding are to name your business, create your logo, and develop your image.

According to the Online Free Dictionary, the word *brand* is "a trademark or distinctive name identifying a product or a manufacturer." An example of a brand is Coca-Cola. The Coca-Cola Company manufactures Coca-Cola soda. The color, the font, and the way It is designed will allow you to know that it is a Coca-Cola product without giving it much thought. It is very important for you to understand colors and color patterns as well because they also have meaning in business.

The company brand often distinguishes itself from another business and represents the organization to the community. A logo or graphic presentation can represent a brand, and it can be evaluated based on the public's awareness of the brand. Branding allows the public to expect consistency in terms of service and/or product offered.

Before ownership of a brand can take place, you must first do your research to ensure no one already has ownership of it. If someone has trademarked or servicemarked your ideal brand, government agencies usually protect it. You can trademark or servicemark your unique and original brand, which attorneys or other firms that specialize in trademarks do.

If you have the time, you can research the desired name of your company and trademark it yourself. However, be aware that the application process to trademark can take up to one year in the United States. Once the trademark process is finalized, you may register your company name with the ™ mark.

Branding is one of the most important aspects in building a business. Developing your brand is building trust between your consumers and you. It is your promise to them that, once they see your brand, they will receive a certain type of product or service. Your brand is the signature of who and what you are, what you have to offer, how you are offering it, and to whom you will be offering it to. With a strategic branding strategy, you will be one step ahead toward completion.

When you begin to brand your business, you must create a logo, a graphic presentation of who and what your business is. It is the foundation of your business and will be integrated onto your signage, brochures, website, and other marketing materials. All of this will be used to communicate who you are as a company or business. Color, symbols, sizes, and styles of various fonts used will all communicate the style, quality, and importance you place on your customers.

Meanings of Color in Business

- Red, a physical color, makes a statement and calls for action. This color is high in energy, and its intensity grabs attention.
- Orange evokes exuberance, fun, and vitality. Optimistic and fun, it suggests affordability.

- Yellow communicates optimism, stimulates our analytical processes, and assists with mental clarity.
- Green is associated with nature, health, and prestige. It is also linked with freshness and newness.
- Turquoise represents open communication and clarity and inspires the same calming and peaceful effects as blue.
- Blue implies honesty, trust, and dependability.
- Indigo represents strength and power. Using this color will send a message of integrity and sincerity. Structural, ritualistic, and routine-based practices utilize this color.
- Purple works well with many colors and suggests wealth, royalty, and creativity.
- Magenta represents spirituality. It encourages a balanced outlook based on practicality and common sense.
- Pink inspires compassion and has a nurturing personality. Women often use this color in business because it also denotes fun and is nonthreatening.
- Gold is associated with wealth, value importance, luxury, and prestige. Generosity, along with wisdom and beauty, can be linked with this color.
- Silver is sophisticated, calming, peaceful, and serene, yet it is an uplifting color with a degree of mystery about it.
- Black denotes power, prestige, and authority. It must be used in moderation because it can be overpowering. Also at the same time, black and white are not true colors in the business arena.
- White implies efficiency and simplicity, professionalism, and order.

- Gray, a neutral color, represents security, and it is a great foundational background for other colors.
- Brown is strong and reliable and represents something being down-to-earth. It conveys simplicity, durability, and stability. Be careful. It can create a negative effect to those who associate brown with dirt or being dirty.

Create Your Logo

Now that you have a good idea about how to use color in business, it will be a great time to study symbolism. When creating the language between you and your potential customer in the form of a logo, ensure it reflects and illuminates the desired outcome you wish to create. You must take time to research what you want in order to effectively communicate what you have to offer. Laying down the groundwork in the creation of your logo may take time, energy, meditation, and consideration for it to convey your message at the magnitude you are hoping for.

After spending time meditating on the vision within you, begin to formulate the idea of your logo by asking yourself a few questions and writing down your answers on paper. Use the following guide to help stimulate the creative juices to flow through the paths of your thoughts as you begin to correlate the vision with the logo. Your logo is a communication tool between you and your potential customers, and it should speak volumes on your behalf when you are not speaking.

The colors of the logo and every stroke of the fonts you use should immediately portray the type of valuable service and product you want to offer. It should engage your customer's emotions on all levels—spiritually, physically, and emotionally. Your logo should paint an optimal scenario of what the consumers' encounter of your company will be. Take care that the logo is not complicated as well, that is, does not involve too much detail, as this may have a backlash affect, causing a potential customer to become overwhelmed with your image. Remember that your logo is a language between you and the eye that beholds it.

Now that you have basic information on the importance of a logo, let us move forward. The naming of the company is equally as important as the logo. The company name is the nail that holds everything else, the box that holds the present, the cup that holds the juice, the first letter in the alphabet, and the map that will lead your customers on that very journey to the desired outcome of closing the sale. Once people hear your business name, a picture should automatically form in their minds.

This image is whatever you want it to be. It should entice your customers to want to know more. Keep it simple and easy to remember. The consumer needs to be able to spell it, pronounce it, and convey what it is to someone else. Who is going to remember a name that is difficult to pronounce, spell, or read?

Now let's get started. Write down your answers to the following questions. Then go back to see if you have created the picture and story that equals your vision. Then have someone else view it and see if it creates the desired effect. Ask someone who will give you his or her most honest opinion.

- What is the name of your company?
- What are your company colors?
- What is your company logo?
- What does your company name mean to you?
- Does the name convey that meaning to others?

- Why did you choose those particular colors? Do they convey the message you want to represent?
- Once you put your logo and name together, what do they say to others?

Now that you have a great business name and logo, be sure to hire a graphic designer who can bring it all together as well as implement the creativity behind your vision that will set you apart from your competition. Once your logo is created, it can help you organize your thoughts. Based on the information you have written above, it's time to solidify your brand and create a vision, mission statement, and motto for your company.

A vision statement is a statement of purpose and the steering wheel of where you are driving your company. It should have the preferred conclusion in mind, ultimately displaying where your company will end up. It identifies the path your company will take as well as the goals it will accomplish.

I like to say the vision is implanted within you and birthed through prayer and/or meditation. This is one of the first things I learned from a leader, who happens to be my pastor and an entrepreneur.

The vision statement must be clear and focused and able to produce insight for those who read it. If you have a team that cannot see your vision at least part of the time, they will not hold the value and will not be able to help you carry it out. So be precise and clear with the outcome desired, and ensure it is attainable in the vision. Those who see this vision statement must be able to trust it, uphold it, and see it as the pot of gold at the end of the rainbow. The vision statement is what the company will become.

Your vision statement may be one statement or a few sentences, but it should hold the component of what it will become. The story of how it will get there belongs to the work of your mission statement. A good vision statement should be broad and used for the long term, and it should not be too general.

Some examples of a vision statement are the following:

- To help provide a clean, friendly environment for our workers
- To sell our products nationwide
- To help produce and deliver quality products through the implementations of systems, structures, and sound, well-communicated policies

Now it's your turn. What is your vision statement?

What Is a Mission Statement?

The mission statement is an announcement that describes what your company and/or organization is working toward. It provides the what, when, how, and why of your company's existence. It should provide clear, logical goals, strategies, and functions as your company's driver. While your vision statement is the vehicle, the mission statement will be the force driving your company toward the fulfillment of your mission's statement. It should include the description of the product or service you produce as well as the demographics it will operate in.

This statement should be communicated and discussed thoroughly with your employees or team members. Write this statement in one sentence that describes the purpose of your company's existence. Be sure every facet of your company is depicted in the mission statement. What is your mission statement?

What Is a Motto?

A motto is a short, likable statement that gives your company recognition in the marketplace. It is part of your brand and can contain something memorable from the mission statement. Your motto, an expressive phrase for your business, should contain a description of your beliefs and ethical stance. It can be used to give your company focus as it strives to reach its goal within the community. It is what the general public will remember about you. The mission statement is a reminder for the employees, and it is okay if the customers don't know or remember it.

However, your clients will remember your motto. When they hear your company's name or see the logo, they should hear the motto as well. For example, the motto of my home health aide company is "We care for you." It tells our clients that we are providing a service with their care in mind. Now write your short motto below, and be sure it essentially communicates what your company is about.

An incomplete or nonexistent motto will cause your company to lose its focus and will fail to catch and retain the community's attention. It should be used consistently to penetrate the minds of your target market. You need time to allow the motto to help build your brand. During the branding process, you are gaining recognition and attention based on the motto. The more expressive you are with the motto, the stronger the brand. What is your motto?

The Vision Board

All great leaders have a vision board. Keeping your vision in front of you will remind you of what you want and when it will happen, and it will reveal the desired outcome. It should contain goals, pictures, resources, and a guide of how you will get there. It predicts the finished product. The vision board reflects the light at the end of the tunnel, and it will produce manifestation because it is always with you, reminding you. It will bring you to a call of action, ignite fire, and create a sense of urgency in you.

The ultimate goal of the vision board is to propel you next to the dimension in your thinking. Without vision or direction, you will travel a road that leads to frustration and eventual chaos. Utilization of a vision board will bring clarity, concentration, and a complete focus on the desired specific life goal of the company. Many people also use the vision board to display the vision of their personal lives.

The vision board will do three things: reinforce what you are speaking; affirm what you are speaking; and keep your focus on what you are speaking.

A vision board coupled with a vision statement will help you believe in the vision, give clarity to the dream, give direction to the concept, and provide daily affirmations. You should spend time investing energy and thought into your vision board. It is a direct communication of your creativity and dreams imparted into you.

Create a Vision Board

To create a vision board, you will need a white board, pictures of what you want to see manifest in your life (which you can take from magazines), and a simple vision.

Write the vision, and make it plain so that those who read it and see it can run with it!

Chapter 4

Business Structures

In this chapter we will briefly look at various business structures. Here you will gain insight into the different structures and learn how they will relate to the type of company you are formulating. It will provide the skeleton or outer shell to the body of your company from a legal and tax viewpoint. Building your company as a corporation will label it as a separate legal entity that has been incorporated either directly through legislation or a registration process established by law. As an incorporated entity, your company has legal rights and liabilities that are distinct from the owners, employees, and shareholders.

Once established as a corporation, you may conduct business as either a profit-seeking business or nonprofit business. In addition to their legal characteristics, registered corporations tend to have limited liability. They are owned by shareholders who can transfer their shares to others. And they are controlled by a board of directors who are normally elected or appointed by the shareholders. The American English Dictionary denotes the word *corporation* as "a large company or business organization."

The law views corporations (as an entity) as legal persons that have many of the same rights and responsibilities as natural people do. Corporations can act and extend their entity rights against real persons and the state, as well as being responsible for human rights violations.

What Is an LLC?

A limited liability company, or LLC, and its structure allows for the combination of the pass-through taxation of a partnership or sole proprietorship with the restricted accountability of a corporation. Like the owners of a sole proprietorship or partnership, the LLC reports business profits or losses on its income tax returns. The LLC itself is not a separate taxable entity like its corporation counterpart; however, its owners are protected from personal liability of business debt and claims. Should a suit arise against the company, only its assets are at risk. The owners' personal assets are not.

New business owners tend to structure their business this way for that reason. You may also form a partnership under this structure. In the LLC, the partners are known as members, and ownership may be divided equally among the members or as they may deem a good fit.

Sole proprietorship is a business entity that is operated and owned solely by the individual who founded it. In this case there is no legal separation between the owner and the company. This simply means that the individual is the business and the business is the individual. The individual is legally responsible for all business conducted and holds all the liability. Your personal assets can and will be attached to your business. Individuals utilize this business structure at a time they are just starting out, but I would not recommend it. Please seek legal counsel in this matter or consult your business tax consultant.

How Will You Structure Your Business?

Will you be a sole proprietor, LLC, partnership, or corporation? The goal for this chapter is to read several books on business structure. Answer the following questions:

- After research, do you understand the basics of the business structure you chose?
- Whom will you obtain as a business tax consultant?
- Have you consulted a business attorney?
- What books on business structures have you read?
  - Book 1
  - Book 2
  - Book 3
  - Book 4
  - Book 5

Partnerships

Partnerships are formed between one or more businesses and/ or individuals where they work together to achieve a common desired outcome or goal. They are, so to speak, "on the same page." They share the same qualities and work ethics as the other and understand, if one doesn't do something, the other will pick up the slack. Much care and thought must be taken when considering a partnership with someone else. Legally, it is like a marriage, and the burden and liability will rest equally on all parties involved.

When considering a partner, one must be a leader, and the other must be a follower. However as partners, the role of leader and follower may invariably change, but it should be clear that, in partnerships, there must be unity in decisions. Each partner shares in the labor, skill, assets, and financials, as well as in the profits and losses equally.

There are three types of partnerships. The information below was taken from the Small Business Administration (SBA) website, sba.gov. I found this website to be very helpful and useful in my own research.

General Partnerships

Assume that profits, liability, and management duties are divided equally among partners. If you opt for an unequal distribution, the percentages assigned to each partner must be documented in the partnership agreement.

Limited Partnerships

Also known as a partnership with limited liability, these are more complex than general partnerships. Limited partnerships allow partners to have limited liability as well as restricted input with management decisions. These limits depend on the extent of each partner's investment percentage. Limited partnerships are attractive to investors with short-term projects.

Joint Ventures

These act as a general partnership, but for only a limited period of time or a single project. Partners in a joint venture can be recognized as an ongoing partnership if they continue the venture, but they must file as such.

Answer the following questions:

- If you decide to have a partnership, who will it be with?
- Does he or she have the finances needed to help you in business?
- Does he or she have the work ethic required to run the business?
- Does he or she possess the education and necessary skills needed to help you in the business?
- Does he or she have good credit? This is vital because his or her financial integrity might affect the outcome of the business.
- What are his or her credentials? Does he or she have a strong knowledge base in the area you specialize in?

When forming a partnership, be sure to include the other person's input in the branding process. This will be a direct reflection of everyone involved; hence everyone involved must line up with the brand.

Chapter 5

Developing the Plan

The groundwork has been laid, the plan has been thought out and processed, and the vision has been written. Now it's time to put together the plan. All businesses start with a good business plan, a written report of attainable goals, and includes why they are attainable, how they will be obtained, and what is needed to get them. This plan may consist of background information on the business, its members, and the rationale behind its formation. The mission, vision, and motto may be included. The demographics of its makeup as well as the marketing plan should be clear, precise, and accurate.

Companies use business plans as organizational tools to obtain capital. Or used internally, they provide a map to where the business is going. They are detail-oriented and include projections of profits anywhere from three to five years. This is important because investors will be looking to see when they should expect a return on their investments. If the plan does not include clear, detailed, goal-oriented factors, it may not be taken seriously and will not provide the desired outcome.

The components of a business plan can include several formats, especially for new companies. They all should include the following information: financing, operations plan, marketing plan, and balanced scorecard.

Financing

This is how the company will obtain and grow its financing. It is the allocation of liability and access attained through certainty and uncertainty. The aim of this section is to price and place value on assets, to determine the risk level and rate of return.

What is needed to start, operate, and maintain the company? This includes the projected budget from three to five years, ways to grow the business financially, and means needed to obtain the goals. There will need to be a plan in place, such as projected payroll, the relationship between the payroll and income earned, taxes, banking and savings, the person or people who will manage it, and ways it will be done. The budget is included in this portion, and it should be very detailed to include supplies needed, equipment, assets, and so forth.

You should at least have basic knowledge of finances as well as money management. It is wise to hire a professional consultant in this area for he or she is trained and qualified to manage this portion of your business. (Hint: although you may wish to hire a professional, it is still wise to have basic knowledge to ensure he or she is performing at the level you need him or her to be.) This portion of the plan should include sales, profits, cash flow, and return on investments.

Operations Plan

This portion of the plan details how the company will operate and what, how, who, and when it will sell or produce. This section is the who, what, where, how, and when of the business. It includes the business locations and human resources needed, the way everyone will be trained, and the employment process.

You might also want include how you will attract and retain new personnel, their skill set requirements, and the team that will manage them. Investors want to know that there are qualified personnel to carry out the functions of the business to make it successful. You should also include troubleshooting. In other words, in case something goes opposite of what is expected, this is how you plan to resolve it when there is minimum risk or loss.

Marketing Plan

This portion will explain the target market, the ways you plan to infiltrate or penetrate the target market, and the demographics of your target market. You will need to do a SWOT analysis for strengths, weaknesses, opportunities, and threats. A PEST analysis checks for political, economic, social, and technological impacts.

Balanced Scorecard

This is the analysis of the impact of achieving objectives from a financial, customer, and internal perspective and of innovation and learning, together with the identification of critical success factors, performance measures, opportunities, and strategies. This portion must include evidence of knowledge of market conditions that include size and structures. The amount of competition is noted here.

You want to indicate the size of the production activity, your potential buyers, and the means of getting the product or service to them. You want to note if company vehicles, equipment, or any outsourcing is necessary to carry out the job. You must include the four Ps of marketing: product, production, pricing, and place (of distribution).

Developing a business plan is very time consuming and the very foundation of your business. Business plans are very effective and can be pricey if you hire a professional. Reading and reviewing various business plans will help you formulate your own.

Your goal for business plan development is to read a certain number of books on business plan developments within a certain time frame.

- Book 1
- Book 2
- Book 3
- Book 4
- Book 5

Answer the following questions:

- What does my operational plan consist of?
- How many employees are needed to complete the task?
- Who will be included on my management team?
- What qualifications are required to be a part of management?
- Which positions will I need to include job descriptions for?

The following is a sample list of each position needed and the job descriptions. This will be the foundation in policy development.

Position 1

Job Description   →   **Education Requirements**

_____   _____

Position 2

Job Description   →   **Education Requirements**

_____   _____

Position 3

Job Description   →   **Education Requirements**

_____   _____

Answer the following questions:

- How will I train the above staff?
- Will training consist of videos, handouts, and so forth?
- What does my application look like? Will I require résumés?
- Will I use a payroll company? If not, who will do my payroll?
- What is the budget for payroll?
- Who will fund the payroll in case I come up short?
- What type of business insurance is needed to legally cover the business?
  - You will need to consult an insurance agent who will be able to tell you the type of insurance needed and/or if you need to be bonded. He or she will also be able to tell you if your business will require worker's compensation insurance, which can be costly.
- Will I need to lease or rent space?
- What is the size requirement for the space?

- What is the budget for the rent or lease?
- How much will be allocated toward utilities?
- What supplies are needed?
- What is the cost needed to obtain/manufacture the supplies or products?
- If vendors are needed, do I have a wholesale supplier?
- Where will I obtain and store my supplies?
- Do I have the necessary software to competently run each department?
- How will I maintain my employee files? Where will they be stored?
  - You will need to keep record of these files for up to seven years based on your governing body.
- Do I have furniture for my business? Is it needed?
- If so, what is the budget and projected cost for it?
  - When it comes to the financials, you want to have a basic understanding of cash flow statements, balance sheets, accounts receivables, and profit and loss statements.
- Have I read books on finances?
  - Book 1
  - Book 2
  - Book 3
  - Book 4
  - Book 5
- Do I have a business checking and/or savings account?
- Do I have—or will I need—a line of credit?
- Do I have three to six months worth of operational expenses saved in case of an emergency?
- How will my services or products be purchased?
- Where will the suppliers come from?

- Have I predicted any weakness that may arise and derived a plan or strategy to overcome the limitations?
- What are the potential downfalls?
- What are all the errors or mishaps that could possibly go wrong?
- What can I do to prevent them from happening?
- If I am unable to prevent it, what will be the solution to overcome them?

Please provide detailed answers to each question. These queries will guide you through the implementation phase of your business development. They will also serve as a handbook during your policy development. Most business owners who do not have the capital to hire the entire team needed in the beginning find themselves administratively running their own companies. It is imperative that you understand the art of problem solving and brainstorming and become solution-oriented.

Chapter 6

Marketing Plan

Marketing is the process of displaying and communicating a product or services. It emphasizes the value of the product or service for influencing the buyer. The desired outcome of marketing is to influence buyer behavior in favor of the company being marketed. Marketing involves these four components: internal, relational-based, integrated, and socially responsive.

For successful marketing, your strategy must involve capturing marketing insights, building a strong brand, connecting with your customers, providing solutions to their needs, effectively communicating your value, determining long-term growth and development, and developing structured plans on how to build. Your marketing strategy should include goals, time frames, places, demographics, and materials needed to influence the buyer market.

A marketing plan involves the actual process and strategies your business will complete in order to reach and influence your targeted customers. The plan should be consistent, and the direction it is headed in must produce growth. Market conditions, competition, and the environment must be included when developing a strategy to market your product or service.

Tactics that may be used include, but are not limited to, the mailing of postcards, pricing changes, product improvements, and so on. You should know what your competitors are offering and how they are presenting it. This will give you an idea of how to set apart your product or service from them.

Marketing strategies involve activities that will make your product or services available to your clients or customers in a way that is satisfying or appealing to them. Numerous and various activities can accomplish this goal, including ensuring the design of the product is desirable; promoting the product or service through public relations, advertisements, and communications; and ensuring consistency pricing and availability of your product or service.

Every business should understand the importance of effective marketing because that is how it distributes its product or service. Careful thought must be taken when developing and implementing your plan. You must also understand the importance of tracking and following your activities to determine your plan's effectiveness.

If it is not producing the desired effect, a change is necessary. If done effectively, marketing will enhance the sale and growth of your company. It will also encourage healthy competition. Not only will your customers know your service and product, your competitors will too.

Advertising

Advertising and marketing are different although people often get the two confused. Advertisement is a nonpersonal persuasive message that is paid, published, and announced by an identified sponsor. The key here is that it is nonpersonal and delivered by a sponsor, such as radio announcements, billboards, newspaper ads, and so forth. Marketing involves the building of a relationship, physical contact, and exchange of information in a strategic way. It entails systematic planning and implementation of the plan. Advertising is a single component of a bigger plan, the marketing plan.

Developing Your Marketing Plan

The goal for this plan will be to read five books on marketing:

- Book 1
- Book 2
- Book 3
- Book 4
- Book 5

Answer the following questions:

- What does my definition of marketing include?
- What is my definition of advertisement?

When creating your marketing plan, ask yourself the following questions:

- What will be the pricing of the product or service?
- What are the competitors' prices for a similar product or service?
- What will make my product or service different?
- How will the product or service meet the customer's needs?
- How will I market this product or service?

- Will I attend events?
- Do I have to utilize speaking engagements?
- Will I use radio, TV, newspaper, flyers, and announcements?
- Will I offer discounts and special prices?
- Who will help with the marketing?
- What is the budget for your marketing?
  - Advertisement will be the largest expense in this plan.
- Will I utilize Internet marketing?
- How will my customers find me on the Internet?
- Will I have a website?
- Will I be listed in an online directory, such as Yellow Book?
- How will clients or customers know I am in town?
- Have I done market research? That is, do I know how my product or service will be accepted among the various demographics?
- What age group will I be targeting?
- Do I know how my target audience receives information?
  - For example, if I want an Internet business, I wouldn't be targeting senior citizens with low education levels who live in a rural area. This population still utilizes paper advertisements.

References

American Psychological Association (APA)
Dictionary.com Unabridged. "Integrity." Accessed September 22, 2015. http://dictionary.reference.com/browse/integrity.

American Psychological Association (APA)
Dictionary.com Unabridged. "Character." Accessed September 22, 2015. http://dictionary.reference.com/browse/character.

American Psychological Association (APA)
Dictionary.com Unabridged. "Morals." Accessed September 22, 2015. http://dictionary.reference.com/browse/morals.